Alison Curtin

To Nora Brett,
for giving me the best start...

2 6
÷
3 ×1
5

Peter the Pea and Polly the Pansie were the best of friends.

They grew up as neighbours and went to the same preschool in the countryside.

They spent their preschool days painting, colouring, playing games outside and making new friends. It was safe to say the Pea and the Pansie loved school.

BIG
SCHOO

The months were starting to fly by, and their preschool teacher Ms Anabelle was speaking to the children about the upcoming graduations from preschool.

"What is a graduation?" asked Peter the Pea.

"A graduation is a very special day where we celebrate the end of your preschool years and wish you well with your new chapter," said Ms Anabelle.

"But where am I going?" asked the Pea.

"Big School!" the other children echoed.

Will i make new friends?
Will i have a nice schoolbag like Pansie?
Will my teacher be nice to me?

Peter the Pea was a little doubtful about his big move but Polly the Pansie on the other hand was excited.

Polly boasted to her friends, "I am going to make lots of new friends at Big School and my Mummy is going to buy me a brand-new schoolbag."

Peter the Pea was a little anxious and uncertain. Questions gathered in his head...

"Will I make new friends?"

"Will I have a nice schoolbag like Pansie?"

"Will my teacher be nice to me?"

At home time, Ms Annabelle told Peter, Polly and their friends that there was an important envelope in their schoolbags to give to Mummy and Daddy.

Peter's mum was so happy to see that she had received an invitation to Peter's Preschool Graduation.

BIG Sc
and
Presc

The next day, Ms Anabelle noticed that Peter the Pea looked worried and decided to have a chat at Circle Time to address the childrens' questions.

She explained that Big School is just like preschool and that the children will still have plenty of time to make friends, play with toys and eat their lunches.

Ms Anabelle explained that the only changes are that the day is longer, and the children in Big School wear a uniform.

Graduation day came and went, and Peter the Pea was feeling better about starting school.

The summer holidays had passed and the first morning of Big School had arrived.

"My tummy feels funny," Peter the Pea said to Mummy Pea.

"Those are called butterflies," Mummy Pea said. "They mean you are excited and maybe a little nervous too," she explained.

As they set off on their walk to the local school hand in hand. Peter smiled as he recognised his friends Alana Aubergine and Ciara Cucumber at the school gates.

Peter suddenly felt brave and said, "I think I am ready now Mummy."

So Mummy Pea walked Peter to the school gate and off he went into the school hall with his new teacher, Ms Felix.

Peter the Pea could not help but wonder where his best friend Polly the Pansie was.

Do you know where she could be?

Polly the Pansie was not feeling so brave anymore. She held her Mummy's hand tightly and did not want to let go. Ms Felix was trying her best to make Polly calm, but she appeared to be quite upset. "Mummy, don't go!" she screamed.

Peter the Pea once again felt brave and walked over to Polly the Pansie.

"Polly, remember when I was nervous about starting Big School? And remember what Ms Anabelle told us? 'We need to remember that Big School is not going to be too different to preschool and we can still have fun!'"

And with that, Polly wiped her eyes and off they went to the classroom.

Ms Felix allowed the two friends to choose a toy from the shelf to play with while the rest of the children arrived, and in the end, they both had a great day.

THE END

Look Out for
More Adventures

The Pea and the Pansie Make New Friends

The Pea and the Pansie go to the Doctor

The Pea and the Pansie go Swimming

The Pea and the Pansie go to the Dentist

About the Author

My name is Alison Curtin, and I am from Youghal in East Cork, Ireland. I am lucky enough to own a preschool in a gorgeous village called Ladysbridge and I consider myself very lucky to be based in such a close-knit community.

I have worked with young children for many years now and I always wanted to write about my experiences in the form of a children's book to hopefully provide comfort during times of change and transition in a child's school life.

First published in paperback by
Michael Terence Publishing in 2023
www.mtp.agency

Copyright © 2023 Alison Curtin

Alison Curtin has asserted the right to be identified as
the author of this work in accordance with the
Copyright, Designs and Patents Act 1988

ISBN 9781800945326

Illustrations by
Tom Burchell

Cover Design
Copyright © 2023 Michael Terence Publishing

Michael Terence
Publishing